SPECTRUM
READERS

MW01133360

BRR!
Arctic
Animals

By Teresa Domnauer

Carson-Dellosa
Publishing

An imprint of Carson-Dellosa Publishing, LLC
P.O. Box 35665
Greensboro, NC 27425-5665

© 2014, Carson-Dellosa Publishing, LLC. Except as permitted under
the United States Copyright Act, no part of this publication may
be reproduced, stored, or distributed in any form or by any means
(mechanically, electronically, recording, etc.) without the prior written
consent of Carson-Dellosa Publishing, LLC. Spectrum is an imprint of
Carson-Dellosa Publishing, LLC.

carsondellosa.com

Printed in the USA. All rights reserved.
ISBN 978-1-4838-0111-7

01-002141120

Some animals are at home in the Arctic.
They hunt, swim, and have babies in this cold, icy land.
Amazing Arctic animals can survive very long winters.

Arctic Fox

A fox is at home
in the Arctic.
In warm seasons,
it has brown fur.
In cold seasons,
its fur turns white
to match the snow.

Polar Bear

A polar bear is at
home in the Arctic.
Its sharp claws
grip the ice.
It hunts for seals.

8

Puffin

A puffin is at home
in the Arctic.
Puffins dive in the
icy ocean.
They flap their wings
under the water.

Walrus

A walrus is at home
in the Arctic.
Thick, fatty skin
keeps it warm.
Walruses rest in
groups called *herds*.

Sled Dog

A sled dog is at home
in the Arctic.
Its tough paws pull
sleds across snow.
A thick coat keeps it warm.

Caribou

A caribou is at home
in the Arctic.

Snowy Owl

A snowy owl is at home in the Arctic. Its white feathers blend in with snow and ice. This protects it from enemies like wolves.

Fur Seal

A fur seal is at home in the Arctic.
It can see and hear very well.
It may stay in the icy ocean for weeks.

Musk Ox

A musk ox is at home
in the Arctic.
Its shaggy coat
covers wool.
In spring, the ox
sheds the wool.

Arctic Wolf

A wolf is at home
in the Arctic.
The Arctic wolf
runs swiftly.
It is a good hunter.

Arctic Tern

A tern is at home
in the Arctic.
It spends summers
in the Arctic.
In winter, it flies to
the South Pole!

26

Narwhal

A narwhal is at home
in the Arctic.
This whale has one
long tusk.
All winter, it lives
below the ice.

Wolverine

A wolverine is at home
in the Arctic.
This fierce animal
has a bushy tail.
It makes its den in
the snow.

Killer Whale

A killer whale is at home in the Arctic. Sharp teeth help it hunt in the ocean. It eats fish, squid, and seals.

BRR! Arctic Animals
Comprehension Questions

1. Which Arctic animals have white coloring?

2. How do a caribou's hooves help it?

3. What happens to the fur of an Arctic fox in winter?

4. How many tusks does a narwhal have?

5. What helps walruses stay warm?

6. What helps a musk ox stay cool in warm weather?

7. Where do Arctic terns live during the summer?

8. What does a polar bear hunt for?

9. How do puffins swim?

10. What do killer whales eat?